Predators in the Wild

Scorpions

by Adele Richardson

Consultant:

Brent E. Hendrixson

Arachnid Biologist & Biology Graduate Student

West Texas A&M University

CAPSTONE
HIGH-INTEREST
BOOKS

an imprint of Capstone Press
Mankato, Minnesota

Capstone High-Interest Books are published by Capstone Press
151 Good Counsel Drive, P.O. Box 669, Mankato, Minnesota 56002
http://www.capstone-press.com

Library of Congress Cataloging-in-Publication Data
Richardson, Adele, 1966–
    Scorpions/by Adele Richardson.
    p. cm.—(Predators in the wild)
    Includes bibliographical references (p. 31) and index.
    Summary: Describes the physical characteristics, hunting methods, and
distribution of scorpions and their relationship with humans.
    ISBN 0-7368-1318-7 (hardcover)
    1. Scorpions—Juvenile literature. [1. Scorpions.] I. Title. II. Series.
QL458.7 .R535 2003
595.4'6—dc21   2001007854

Editorial Credits
Carrie Braulick, editor; Karen Risch, product planning editor; Timothy Halldin,
    series designer; Gene Bentdahl, book designer and illustrator; Jo Miller,
    photo researcher

Photo Credits
Ann & Rob Simpson, 14
Comstock, background elements
David Liebman, 17 (upper left, upper right, lower left)
Digital Vision, 15, 17 (lower right)
G. & C. Merker/Visuals Unlimited, 10
James E. Gerholdt, 6, 22
Joe McDonald, 16, 27, 28
John D. Cunningham/Visuals Unlimited, 21
Robert & Linda Mitchell, cover, 8, 9, 11, 12, 18, 20, 24

Table of Contents

Features

Common name: Scorpion

Scientific name: Scorpiones

Length: Scorpions usually are .5 inch (1.3 centimeters) to 8 inches (20 centimeters) long.

Life span: Most scorpions live two to 15 years.

Habitat: Scorpions live on every continent except Antarctica. Most scorpions live in deserts. They also live in rain forests, prairies, and woodlands.

Prey:

Scorpions eat mainly insects, spiders, and other scorpions. Large scorpions sometimes eat small lizards, frogs, snakes, and mice.

Eating habits:

Scorpions grab their prey with claws called pincers. Most scorpions then kill the prey by stinging it with their tails. All scorpions spit digestive juices onto their prey. They then suck the prey into their mouths.

Behavior:

Scorpions are solitary animals. They live and hunt alone. Most scorpions are nocturnal. These scorpions hunt at night.

In This Chapter:

* Scorpions have an exoskeleton.

* Scorpions are arachnids.

* The largest scorpions live in Africa and Asia.

Chapter 1

Scorpions

Scorpions are related to spiders. They have pincers and stinging tails. Scientists believe that scorpions have lived on Earth for more than 400 million years.

Scorpion Species

Scorpions are in a group of animals called arthropods. Arthropods do not have skeletons inside their bodies. They have outer skeletons called exoskeletons. Their bodies are divided into sections.

Scientists divide the arthropod group into classes. Scorpions belong to the class Arachnida. Spiders, mites, and ticks also are

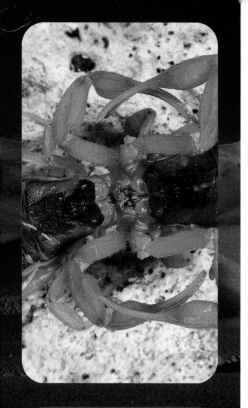

in this class. All arachnids have eight legs and two main body sections.

Scientists divide the Arachnida class into orders. Scorpions make up the order Scorpiones. This order includes more than 1,500 species. More than 90 species live in the United States. Many scientists believe that there are hundreds more scorpion species that have not yet been discovered.

Appearance

Scorpions have flat, narrow bodies. Two pincers are attached to the front of their head. Scorpions use the pincers to catch prey.

Scorpions have camouflage coloring. Most scorpions are a shade of black, brown, or yellow. The colors blend with their surroundings.

Some scorpions are a shade of yellow.

A scorpion's long tail is divided into segments. A sharp, hollow stinger is at the end of a scorpion's tail. The stinger points toward the head. A scorpion often stings prey caught in its pincers with its tail.

African emperor scorpions are one of the largest species.

Size

Scorpions vary in size. Several small species grow only to about .5 inch (1.3 centimeters) long. The largest scorpions are Asian forest and African emperor scorpions. They can grow to more than 8 inches (20 centimeters) long.

The largest scorpion in North America is the giant desert hairy scorpion. It can grow to about 5 inches (13 centimeters) long.

Scorpions shed their skin to grow. Young scorpions usually molt within two weeks after birth. Scorpions often shed their skin more than five times before they are fully grown. Scorpions usually reach their full size within two to six years.

Young

Female scorpions give birth between three and 18 months after mating. A female scorpion may give birth to as many as 25 to 35 young.

The young scorpions climb onto the mother's back. They do not eat. Instead, they receive energy from fat stored in their bodies. The young scorpions can care for themselves after about two weeks.

In This Chapter:

* Most scorpions ambush prey.

* Scorpions capture prey with their pincers.

* Scorpions can sense prey's movement.

Chapter 2

The Hunt

Scorpions are called carnivores because they eat only meat. They often eat spiders, insects, and other scorpions. They may eat snails and earthworms. Large scorpions sometimes eat frogs, small lizards, snakes, and mice.

Hunting Habits

Most scorpions are nocturnal. These scorpions hunt mainly at night. Scorpions

Many bark scorpions hunt more actively than other species.

often rest in underground holes called burrows or under rocks when they are not hunting.

Most scorpions ambush prey. These scorpions are known as sit-and-wait predators. They often stand still at their burrow's entrance and wait for prey to pass by. They grab prey with their pincers as it travels near them.

Other scorpions such as bark scorpions are active while they hunt. These scorpions grab prey with their pincers after they locate it.

Scorpions hunt more when the weather is warm than they do in cold weather. Scorpions are cold-blooded. Their body temperature changes according to their surroundings. Scorpions that become too cold may have trouble moving around.

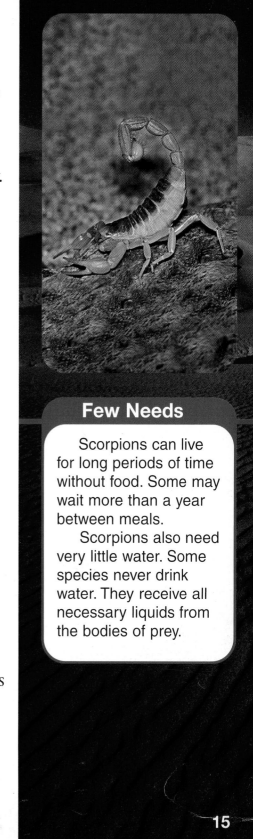

Few Needs

Scorpions can live for long periods of time without food. Some may wait more than a year between meals.

Scorpions also need very little water. Some species never drink water. They receive all necessary liquids from the bodies of prey.

Scorpions have hairs on their legs to help them sense prey.

Senses

Scorpions have sense organs to help them hunt. They have a tiny organ on each leg to help them feel vibrations in the ground. These organs help scorpions feel prey moving from as far as several feet or meters away.

Tiny hairs cover scorpions' legs and pincers. The hairs help scorpions feel air movement to detect animals moving near them.

Scientists are not certain how well scorpions can see. Some scorpion species do not have eyes. Many scientists believe that scorpions with eyes can see shadows in very low levels of light. These scorpions may even be able to see shadows made by starlight.

Crickets

Spiders

Cockroaches

Other Scorpions

In This Chapter:

* Many scorpions inject venom into prey.

* Scorpions spit digestive juices onto prey.

* Venom attacks the prey's nervous system.

Chapter 3

The Kill

Scorpions use their pincers and tails to catch and kill prey. Their tails contain a substance called venom. The venom kills prey.

Scorpions spit digestive juices onto prey. These juices break down the prey before scorpions eat it.

Striking Prey

A scorpion prepares to strike as soon as it senses prey. It opens up its sharp pincers and curls its tail over its back.

Some scorpions have very strong pincers. These scorpions may rarely sting prey. Instead,

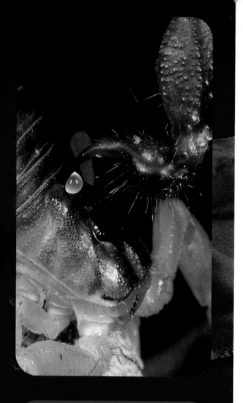

they hold the prey with their pincers and chew off tiny pieces with their mouth parts. Scorpions with weak pincers almost always sting. They rely on the venom in their tails to kill prey.

Venom

Glands in a scorpion's tail make venom. Small tubes called ducts then carry the venom to the stinger.

A scorpion whips its curled tail forward to sting prey. The venom flows into prey through side openings on the stinger. The venom attacks the prey's nervous system. This system controls the body's actions. The prey's major organs stop working and it soon dies.

Antivenin

Scientists use scorpion venom to make a medicine called antivenin. Doctors use antivenin to treat people who are stung by scorpions.

Scientists inject small amounts of scorpion venom into horses to make antivenin. Over time, the horses build up a defense against the venom in their blood. Scientists then use parts of this blood to make antivenin.

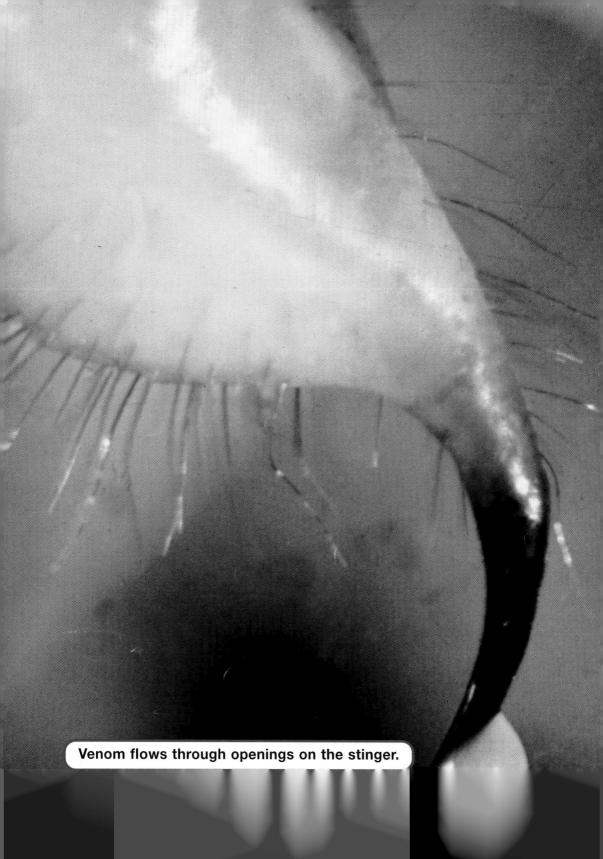

Venom flows through openings on the stinger.

Scorpions suck prey into their mouths.

Eating Prey

A scorpion often tears prey into tiny pieces with its pincers. The scorpion places the pieces into a pile and spits digestive juices onto them. The juices break down the prey's body. The prey becomes soft and sticky. The scorpion then sucks the pieces into its mouth.

Scorpions with strong pincers sometimes eat their prey while it is still alive. These scorpions hold the prey in their pincers. They spit digestive juices onto it. They then chew off bits of the prey's body.

Scorpions eat slowly. They often spend several hours eating one meal.

Myth versus Fact

Myth: All scorpions can kill people.

Fact: Only about 25 scorpion species have venom that can kill people.

Myth: A young scorpion's sting is more harmful than an adult scorpion's sting.

Fact: An adult scorpion can kill prey more easily than a young scorpion can. An adult is able to inject more venom into prey.

Myth: Scorpions are insects.

Fact: Scorpions are arachnids. Arachnids have eight legs and two main body sections. Insects have six legs and three body sections.

In This Chapter:

*   Most scorpions live in deserts.

*   Scorpions may sting to defend themselves.

*   Scorpion venom can help treat illnesses.

Chapter 4

In the World of People

Scorpions have a large range. They live on all continents except Antarctica. Scorpions live in many habitats. Most scorpions live in deserts. Some live in woodlands, rain forests, or prairies. Others live in mountains or along coasts. Scorpions may live near or in people's homes.

Scorpions as Prey

Scorpions are prey to some animals. Lizards, frogs, snakes, and spiders hunt scorpions. Animals such as monkeys and coyotes also

Yellow represents the scorpion's range.

hunt scorpions. Owls and bats may swoop down and eat scorpions.

Scorpions often sting to defend themselves against predators. The stings do not kill all animals that attack scorpions. But they can hurt a large predator.

A scorpion has other defenses. Its body is covered in a hard exoskeleton. The exoskeleton protects the soft organs inside a scorpion's body during an attack. A scorpion's camouflage coloring helps hide it from predators. A dark scorpion blends with dirt or rotting leaves. A light-colored scorpion often blends easily with sand.

Scorpion Stings

Scorpions usually sting people only when they are alarmed. Scorpion stings can be very painful. They often hurt for a few hours.

Most scorpion stings are not dangerous. But about 25 species of scorpions can kill people with their venom. The only species living in the United States that can be life-threatening to people is the bark scorpion. These scorpions live in Arizona, western New Mexico, and parts of Nevada, Utah, and California.

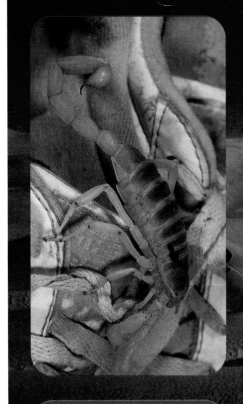

Camping

Campers in scorpion habitats sometimes take precautions to protect themselves from scorpion stings. They may shake out their clothes, shoes, and sleeping bags before using them. In the mornings, they may roll up their sleeping bags and place them above the ground.

Scorpions may live in wood piles.

Living with Scorpions

Scorpions live in many of the same places that people do. Some people take precautions to keep scorpions out of their homes. They may avoid piling rocks or wood near their houses. Scorpions often live or rest under rocks or wood piles.

Some people place smooth ceramic tiles around their homes. Scorpions cannot easily walk over the tiles.

Scorpion Benefits

Many people are afraid of scorpions. But scorpions can help people. Some people have sudden attacks called strokes that affect the brain. Strokes can leave people unable to move some body parts. Scientists made a medicine from scorpion venom that helps people recover from strokes.

In the future, medicine made from scorpion venom may help people recover from diseases that affect the immune system. This system helps people fight off diseases. Some scientists believe this medicine may help people with diseases such as cancer.

antivenin (ant-ee-VEN-in)—a medicine made from scorpion venom that is used to treat scorpion stings

burrow (BUR-oh)—a hole in the ground in which an animal lives

camouflage (KAM-uh-flahz)—coloring or covering that makes animals, people, and objects look like their surroundings

carnivore (KAR-nuh-vor)—an animal that eats meat

digest (dye-JEST)—to break down food so that it can be used by the body

exoskeleton (eks-oh-SKEL-uh-tuhn)—a bony or hard covering on the outside of an animal

nocturnal (nok-TUR-nuhl)—active at night

organ (OR-guhn)—a part of the body that performs a certain job; a person's major organs include the heart and lungs.

pincer (PIN-sur)—a claw used to grasp and hold prey

To Learn More

Lassieur, Allison. *Scorpions: the Sneaky Stingers.* Animals in Order. New York: Franklin Watts, 2000.

Murray, Peter. *Scorpions.* Plymouth, Minn.: Child's World, 1997.

Rankin, Wayne, and Jerry G. Walls. *Tarantulas and Scorpions.* Basic Domestic Reptile and Amphibian Library. Philadelphia: Chelsea House, 1999.

Useful Addresses

American Museum of Natural History
Central Park West at
    79th Street
New York, NY 10024-5192

American Tarantula Society
P.O. Box 756
Carlsbad, NM 88221-0756

Sonoran Arthropod Studies Institute
P.O. Box 5624
Tucson, AZ 85703-0624

Internet Sites

ASU: Ask A Biologist—Not So Scary Scorpions
http://lsvl.la.asu.edu/askabiologist/research/
    scorpions

DesertUSA—Scorpions
http://www.desertusa.com/oct96/du_scorpion.html

Scorpions
http://www.szgdocent.org/ff/f-scorp.htm

Index